THE MYSTERY

BEHIND

GOOGLE MAPS RANKING

&

How to Rank Your Business Higher

By

Qamar Zaman

ISBN 978-1-7355297-1-4

Copyright 2020 © Leeds Press Corp
Cover copyright 2020 © Leeds Press Corp
Cover Design by Leeds Graphics.
Written by Qamar Zaman
Edited by Tara Pollnitz
Final Edits & Formats by Leeds Press Corp Team

www.Leedspublishing.com
Twitter.com/lc3publishing
Instagram.com/lc3publishing
Facebook.com/lc3publishing

LC3 PUBLISHING
LC3 PUBLISHING is an imprint of LEEDS PRESS CORP. Name and Logo is a trademark of LC3 PUBLISHING. The publisher is not responsible for websites (or their content) that are not owned by the publisher LEEDS PRESS SPEAKERS AGENCY provides a wide range of authors for speaking events. To find out more; info@leedspress.com or call 323-230-0062
Printed in the United States of America.
Copyright 2020 © Qamar Zaman
ISBN 978-1-7355297-1-4

Google Map Marketing

"Engage with customers on Google for free", Google Leverage Google MAP for free using Google Business Profile on Google My Business that will help you drive customers looking for your product and services. Create relationships creating engagement with local customers across Google Search and Maps.

Qamar Zaman, Google MAP Expert

Certified Google Partner

Dedication

This book is dedicated to all business owners who are trying to survive during the pandemic.

Acknowledgments

My Team

Agnes Zang, KISS PR

Tara Pollnitz, KISS PR

Dimitry S, KISS PR

My Clients

To all KISS PR Story clients who continue to help me.

Preface

This little guide is no dissertation and no work of profound metaphysics. It is written with an open eye on the possible and practical evolution of the internet. It has no pretensions to scholarship. I have written this booklet as a labor of love for the receptive, candid and positive minds. In my perception, "brand trust" is the future of search engine optimization. SEO is not what most unethical marketing companies are using to take hard-earned money from business owners. Search engine optimization is always creating value-based content that gets shared and adds value to the end-user who consumes the content. I believe that if business leaders don't take the time to understand the foundation, they will continue to be manipulated by unethical marketing companies.

I have always felt convinced and advocated that if we do not adapt to expertise, we can't build authority, and we will never garner the trust of Google.

Qamar Zaman

Contents

Introduction

"Organic & Successful SEO is not about fooling Google.
You must consider Google as your partner."

Qamar Zaman

I have worked on over 1000+ SEO projects comprising of various industries for over 18 years. You can visit the relevant pages on my website to get a feel of the type of SEO solutions I offer: https://kisspr.com.

A lot of people have a passion for initiating a business and wanting to build something from the ground up. We are living in in during difficult times during the pandemic. Most business are suffering and finding your business on Google MAP is more important than ever. In this rapidly changing competitive world, you must convey your business's story and purpose well. You must pivot your marketing strategies ranging from how you portray your business online to how to create visibility for your brand through keywords.

All these years of running websites that provide services for small business to identify their audience, I have seen that success is impossible if SEO and good website designing is compromised. Listen, I have seen plenty of small businesses build websites without considering the 'vibe' and feel of their business. This doesn't help convey their values.

What defines your business? What is your brand voice? You must nail these in the head before developing a website. You can target the right audience when potential customers are looking at content that reflects your brand's values. The most important thing to keep in mind is that the website experience should be top-notch for the customers. It shouldn't be lagging, unappealing, and untrustworthy.

The next best thing is intent of prospect. The new SEO is about the story you tell. If you prospects don't like you, they will not trust you, and to be liked, you must be trusted. Let me introduce myself! My name is Qamar Zaman. Most of my friends tend to call me "Q," which cuts them some slack, I believe. I am based in the United States, and my clients are spread all around Dallas, Chicago, San Francisco, New York

City, New Jersey, Houston, Phoenix, Salt Lake City, North and South Carolinas, Michigan, Los Angeles, and San Diego, The Cayman Islands, and Canada.

I started my company as a website design studio back in 2002 from Grand Cayman after spending 15 years in corporate IT departments of international banks and software companies. Some of these brands included Chase Manhattan now Chase, The Radio Shack, Motorola, and Oracle. In the same year, I helped businesses of all sorts with their website design and marketing needs.

After a while, I took a particular interest in search engine optimization since I needed to find a way to be found online, so I could grow my website design studio. With some of the few friends who worked with me at Silicon Valley, I started to build relationships with search engine coordinators and learned SEO from some of the best minds. The tips and tricks I learned throughout the process still stay with me, and still lend a hand in developing strategies for my current company. I offer various SEO solutions for businesses, especially the aspiring ones, to attract the right target audience and utilize accurate keywords.

One of the SEO masterminds who I learned from was Eric Ward. He used to have a newsletter that I subscribed to for $9 per month. Eric would send tips and unique and interesting ideas in his letter, which I would use to rank my website. Much to my surprise, it started to work like magic! Eric also offered a $300 per month 1-1 coaching call, which lasted for about half an hour. This wasn't a huge sum of money in 2004, but it wasn't economical at the same time, especially for a start-up like me. But, I somehow knew I had to spend that money, so I did.

I can say with confidence that spending $300 per month on a PayPal subscription was the best decision ever. Every month, I would wait anxiously for Eric's web conference call. He taught me some of the most mind-blowing aspects of SEO, but he left the world too soon. On October 16th, 2017, he passed away, leaving me and the SEO industry behind. It was the saddest time of my life, but it made me wonder. The SEO principals that I learned from him are still reflected in my practice of SEO.

The Importance of Website and Digital Marketing and

Why Do Companies Fail to Grasp It?

The reason why I decided to breathe life into this book is to remind all start-up owners that starting a business is a rollercoaster journey. You're met with an unreal amount of highs and lows, but success only comes to those who know what is best for their business, especially in a world dominated by technology. Those who aim to perfect their online presence will be prosperous. My purpose is to remind you of the importance of Google and how it can make or break your business.

A website is a crucial tool for a business. Whenever I click a site, I always try to see how easy the website is to navigate or whether it provides me all the information I need right on the spot. But I also rely on the website to provide me a glimpse of the brand. What is it about? Everything ranging from the layout to the logo, all of it should reflect your brand and your brand only. This allows customers to see what sets you apart from the rest. Then, I'll judge whether that uniqueness is beneficial to me or not. Hence, here, the importance of targeting the right people chimes in.

When you are thinking about starting a new website design project, whether it is a new design or a re-design, you have to remember that the website is an extension of your online presence.

If you are going to start a law firm, you will most likely begin by renting an office. You may lease your place based on your needs, so you have your own sign as people visit your law office. There will be a receptionist by the entrance to greet your clients. You will also need a room for each attorney. The rooms allocated to them will depend on the seniority of each lawyer. Some will get a window office while the junior associates will have to make do with a cubical.

The office will also require a conference room and a break room, and any other law firm essentials. Finally, you would want your law firm in a building that has the best entrance. You would want elevators to show off your status in the marketplace. This is the process of designing a physical office for your company, but the same can be said for your website as well.

You need to choose a logo, colors, and pages for each practice area that match the look and feel of your office. The quality of the pictures should be high-quality, so your clients can see your beautiful office. This procedure is to convey your brand values and what you can offer as a brand. With the right aesthetic, you build a brand identity.

Once your law firm has a beautiful office and a gorgeous website, which is both desktop and mobile-friendly, you're on your way towards a successful business journey. However, you want to make sure that your site is not an expensive billboard, which no one lifts their head up to gaze. That is where you need to think about a marketing strategy to help you identify your potential customers and lure them in.

SEO will be your best partner. Currently, Google is one the most sought-after search engine, and most of your customers will be lurking about on Google. SEO makes your web page easy to find and clickable, meaning your website ranks higher, so more people consider it to be trustworthy. It is easy to convince customers to click your website when you're ranking high in organic search. Many people check out the first page of Google while completely disregarding the next. So, even if your page lands top on the second page, you still lack significantly as compared to the techniques used by your competitors.

To start off with SEO, you must first understand what is your customer searching for? You can take out a plethora of keywords by figuring out the most common way people search for your business. For example, you can search a phrase relating to your website. 'The best law firm in Los Angeles' could be a phrase to search for. Afterward, you can skim through the search results to see that 'Los Angeles law firm' is common in all searches, hence, adding it to your keyword list.

That's how it all begins. There are innumerable ways to conduct keyword searches. You're supposed to make lists of relevant terms and seed keywords, find long-tail keywords, and utilize keyword tools such as Google AdWords, etc. the list is endless. Keyword searching is important, but so is developing a website catering to SEO.

It should be user-friendly, especially mobile-friendly so that the bounce rate – potential customers leaving and not navigating the other pages on your site – decreases. Google also considers lagging pages to be poor, and as your bounce rate is high, Google would find it difficult to rank your website because of less credibility. All the while, the website content should consist of keywords that are relevant and accurate instead of stuffing various keywords relating to the topic. If there are too many keywords, Google suspects the credibility of your content, and it may not rank as high as you had expected because of that.

Social media also plays a huge part in influencing buyer's behavior, so putting your social media buttons on your website is a necessity. Putting a URL link in a social media bio can end up as a link – detected by Google. But links shared on social media are generally just no-follow ones. Social media marketing is second best after SEO because it allows customer engagement and helps locate more customers easily and quickly. You can target clientele using demographics through any metric, but it can get competitive if you don't convey your brand image uniquely.

Most small businesses see the dirt in the absolute first step by not developing a website that reflects the brand's image. The rest simply follows. If this is done correctly, all that you require is the marketing strategies that small businesses often screw up. Most fail to make changes in their SEO content and meet the changing demands of Google. Even if they have SEO in check, the quality of the content can also affect the conversion rate. Is your content conveying the right idea? Does it offer value? What would make the visitors click your website again? SEO itself is vital, but so is ensuring everything around it is kept in check.

Starting a business is becoming the norm but stabilizing one and achieving success is difficult in this competitive world. The only way to ensure success is through developing a compelling online presence paired with digital marketing strategies that make one stand out as quickly as a snap of fingers. Are you ready to dig deeper into the intriguing yet cut-throat world of business?

How Can Every Business Owner Dominate Google Map Rankings Ethically

In this era of digitalization, the market is no longer restricted to conventional mediums or the local market. To ensure a healthy share in the market, it is mandatory that business owners take all measures to increase brand awareness amongst their target audience through any and all means possible.

If you want to boost your sales and want to stay ahead of your competition, the digital sphere is the first place you have to mark your robust presence.

These days it is all about making use of big data to understand your customer and market your brand using a target-based approach. If you are a local business owner with limited resources or a medium enterprise looking to expand its customer base using a marketing technique that is highly effective, then this chapter has the perfect solution for you.

When it comes to searching for anything online, we are all aware of Google's supreme dominance and improvement. It certainly wants to make everyone happy to ensure its own success. Ranked as the most visited multi-platform web properties in the United States, Google has 246 million1 users in the US alone. This denotes the excessive usage of the search engine.

Google offers multiple services and tools to help the business owners to market their goods and services in a more efficient manner. You get better results in the lesser budget.

Google Map Rankings has become one of the necessary ways to expand your customer base and making your business successful in the long run.

What is Google My Business (GMB)?

Google My Business essentially is an interface that allows you the business owner or entrepreneur to take the reins of how your business is going to be displayed on all of the Google platforms. It offers the user a brief about your company and the social proof 2 (reviews) it has received from the customers. Google My Business, or GMB, is Google's one of the tools that promise to improve your business' visibility in your locality as well as to the global audience.

---

[1] https://www.statista.com/topics/1001/google/

[2] https://en.wikipedia.org/wiki/Social_proof

In the online present world, if you want to make your business successful, you have to tap the digital platform. No matter at what scale your business is if you want to retain the competency, online visibility is a must. When you utilize Google My Business service, it marks your business online and you get a claim on the GMB page. Once you have claimed the page, you need to optimize it to make the best use of it and eventually get a higher ranking on the Google Maps and search engine.

To help you with the process, I have developed an infallible strategy for the maintenance of your GMB page. A well-maintained and diligently optimized GMB page can definitely boost your ranking on the Google Maps and bring your business the best visibility on the search engine. So, let's get started with the steps. Since Google will continue to modify its systems and user interface, I have also included a link towards the end of this book so you can always use an updated version with audio, video and text based blogs and notes for your easy access. We have also included direct access to our 24/7 online support system so you can ask questions. Enjoy!

Know Your Audience

You will not be able to make any marketing technique successful unless you treat your customer as the ultimate preference. If they are happy, your business will boom. So, the first step to make your business number one in the Google Maps Rankings is to understand your audience. Every strategy you design to boost your company sales should revolve around your intended audience. Check audio notes on (WHO) step 1 with accompanying online notes.

Now, the most important question is how you will know your audience. Well, the answer to this question lies with Google. It has several tools and services that can provide you with adequate insight into the online behavior of the intended user. You can access to *Google Keyword Planner Tool* through Google Ads account. This tool can help you find the keywords that users are using to search particular things relevant to your business. (See the link in the footer).

The Google Keyword Planner Tool

For instance, if you are a lawyer based in Michigan, you can check multiple keywords like: "Michigan lawyer," "lawyer in

Michigan," "legal help, Michigan," "law firm near me in Michigan." The Google Keyword Planner Tool will give you an insight into how often these words are used in your targeted area. This way you will know what sort of keywords you can use in your content and page to improve its ranking.

Build Your Google My Business Page

Technically, this should be the first step in the process. We have kept it on second deliberately to emphasize on the fact that your preference has to understand your audience or the user first. Only then will you be able to develop an efficient GMB page that is also relevant.

To get your GMB page, you have to register your business and set up a Google My Business account. You can also claim your current business page. When you pursue the GMB site for claiming your business, it shows you a listing of businesses. You have to enter the basic and highly accurate information about your business. This ensures that your business details do not overlap with any existing company and your individuality is maintained. You'll know whether or not your business is in the listing.

You'll be asked to fill the information related to your business and its nature of service. Make sure to be accurate, comprehensive and avoid any grammatical mistakes. There will be the option of business categories – pick the one that is most relevant to your service. Remember that you can always edit your information. It is important that you keep it timely updated and regularly monitored.

The second stage in this process, once you have created the account is the verification of your Google My Business listing. This is important for your online visibility. Once you have made the account, Google will send you a mail to your mailing address that you have already provided. This step is crucial for the verification of your business. You cannot access your GMB page unless it is verified by Google. This may take a week's time after which you'll receive a postcard with a verification code that you've to enter in your page.

Optimize Your GMB Page

Once your business is live, the next step on the list is the optimization of your Google My Business page. Optimization plays an instrumental role in boosting online visibility. It helps you attract a significant amount of visitors. Efficient optimization brings relevant and quality traffic to your website or page.

To optimize your page, information is the first thing you need to work on. Make sure you have accurate details in your profile. Choose the business category carefully. State exactly what your business nature is and what market you deal in. You'll only get relevant traffic if you've mentioned the right details.

Also, your ranking on Google Maps gets directly influenced by the website URL of your Google business page. Google uses your website to make associations with Google Map listings. It utilizes elements like keyword target and business category relevance to equate with user's queries. This impacts your overall ranking.

This makes it necessary for you to optimize the homepage of your website. Careful keyword selection is the foundation of effective optimization. Choose the keywords that are relevant to your business category and relatable to your audience. Once you have chosen the right keywords, the second most important thing to do is their correct placement on your homepage.

The best way to get the top ranking on Google Maps is through placing the keywords in significant locations. Title tags, description tags, onsite content, and citations are primary locations to consider. If you are a California-based financial planner, Google can give you a higher ranking if your title tag says: "Fischer Financial Planning California | Your Wealth Deserves a Plan." This tag immediately shows the basics of your business. Your business name, domain, and the area of practice are clearly stated.

Similarly, having the keyword placed in the description and content gives your landing GMB page more relevance factor. When you place keywords in certain locations, it makes it easier for Google to pull your data and give the page a better ranking.

Besides keywords, you also have to ensure that your website remains updated and offers a productive experience to the user. Keep the basic information visible to the viewer at every page. This includes your business name, address and contact details.

You can use content marketing to ensure that your blog remains updated and has a regular fresh posting of targeted keywords. This will have a positive impact on your online visibility.

Google SEO / Webpage Optimization is all about making your GMB page relevant and enabling for the user. Once you are able to keep it efficiently optimized, you'll see a boost in your business' position on Google Map Rankings.

Cater to Diverse Mediums

Optimizing your GMB page for multiple devices can help you receive a higher ranking on Google Maps. According to CIODive, up to 70% of web traffic happens on mobile devices. This makes it a necessity for you to ensure that your website has a competent and responsive design for mobile users.

Implement a responsive web design that allows easy browsing experience and automatically adjusts to any device it is accessed through by the user.

AMP (Accelerated Mobile Pages) is an initiative developed by Google that can help you make a more mobile-friendly web content. You can use this service to improve search engine ranking. Once you've implemented the AMP markup, your business will be included in Google's SERP's, above search results and sometimes even higher than the paid results.

Remove the unnecessary content from the page to improve mobile user's experience. This includes eliminating blank spaces, irrelevant content, and media. Pages with heavy content take more time to load, negatively affecting the user experience. Keep the design simple and content highly relevant to decrease website load time. Quality images are mandatory for user engagement. So, when you are working on web design, make sure that you add high-quality images. Compressed images take up less space and make it a win-win situation for both you and the user.

When working on a mobile-friendly design for your GMB page, incorporating data in a structured manner can give you surprising results. There are plug-ins that allow you to structure your data in a manner that whenever a query is searched by the user, your website can emerge among top results outranking other websites.

Niche Business Citations

A citation is any online mention of your business name, address and phone number on any other website(s). It can be listed on any online source that has a high Local SEO Authority level. In the local rankings, citations play a huge role in improving your position. The local SEO citations boost your website's authority. Resultantly, your search engine ranking position (SERP) rankings increase within the targeted location.

Citations validate your business and increase your credibility in the local search. The format in which you offer your business information contributes to the reliability factor for the search engines as they filter through the internet. When you offer complete data about your business, it ascertains that you are a legitimate business. Hence, you are pushed above on the search results.

Business citations have a greater share when it comes to the factors influencing the local ranking. However, there are certain aspects that have an important role in determining a positive contribution of business citations in SEO efforts. Firstly, you are likely to have a higher rank than your competitors if your citations are higher in number than that of your competitors. Secondly, Google has more confidence in the citations that are available from trustworthy and well-indexed sites. So, ensure that you choose the sites carefully for citations.

Lastly, it is important that you have citations with the local authority on the location where you're targeting. For instance, having your citation mentioned in Yelp can help boost your local visibility.

Another important thing to improve your ranking on Google Maps through citations is to ensure that all your citations are consistent. They must be in the same sequence with the same address and phone number that you used to register and verify your Google My Business page.

When you have your citations on different trusted sites, it shows that you are part of a community. This is something Google appreciates and improves your ranking in the search results.

Value Reviews

Reviews have played an important part for decades to improve client servicing and boosting sales. Happy customers are key to a successful business. You'll only be able to retain happy customers if you make them feel valued. This happens when you encourage them to offer feedback and you give consideration to what they say.

When it comes to Google Maps Rankings, feedback and reviews are of tremendous value. While there are a lot of other factors involved in search rankings, customer reviews symbolize trustworthiness. They can give you a significant competitive edge and raise your visibility in the search results.

Google looks for certain signals that help the search engine decide whether or not your site is worth a rise in ranking or not. Reviews are an endorsement of trust that assures the search engines about your website.

Reviews confirm that not only your business is legitimate but is approved by the customers, too. Therefore, as a reward, you are given better visibility.

Now what matters is how you manage these reviews. It is important that you know when and where they appear. There are several review sites like Yelp and TripAdvisor that send you a notification whenever a user reviews your page. You can also get paid service for online reputation monitoring. But once you have your GMB page, customers can review you there. You must monitor all the reviews and respond with quality responses accordingly.

When replying to reviews, it is important to have a strong customer service attitude that reflects professionalism. The writing style needs to be friendly. Writing stoically appears to be more offensive. You have to make the customer feel valued for taking out their time to offer you their feedback.

Reviews can be good or bad. You have to deal with both of them carefully. The staff member who is responding to the review must have the authority to resolve the complaints. This will add immediate problem-resolving quality to your service, making a positive contribution to your online reputation.

Negative reviews can be fearsome. They can affect your Google Maps ranking substantially and also pose a negative image for potential customers. But if you know how to manage negative reviews, you will be able to avoid the associated pitfalls.

It is a known fact that a healthy portion of reviews is unauthentic. Agencies are paid to write good or bad reviews for companies. It could be your competitor carrying out the propaganda to tarnish your online image to decrease your ranking. Bearing this possibility into consideration, you have to take measures that can filter out the fake reviews.

You can do this by encouraging the reviewers to post with original names with their reviews. You can also evaluate the language and tone used in the reviews to determine whether or not they are authentic.

For instance, a review with overly negative words and bashing is likely to be false. If a large number of reviews are posted within a short period of time, it indicates a deliberate attempt to sabotage your service's reputation and online ranking.

For legitimate negative reviews, you should shape a careful response that acknowledges the feedback of the customer and also depicts your concern regarding their experience. Reviews are all about the right way of managing. If you know how to handle them correctly, they can play a significant role in bringing to the top of the Google Map Rankings.

Remain Active

This step towards making your business lead in the Google Maps Rankings is to retain a robust online presence. Keeping your website updated with fresh content with optimally positioned keywords can help you improve your rank on Google Maps and retain the top position.

The content can be in multiple formats. You can set up a blog and post relevant articles regularly with the right keywords to ensure Google that your website is timely updated. You can also share the experience of your customers to boost user engagement on your page and offer insight into the service(s) you offer.

You've to remain consistent in your posting. Having an active blog is the easiest way to keep your website current and relevant. You can draft a schedule for posting updates or blogs and then stick to it. Google appreciates consistency and creativity. It will ultimately improve your ranking on all its products if you are successful in assuring the search engine that your content is relevant to the readers.

Feature your blog content using GMB post.

Getting a high ranking on Google Maps is achieved through strategically planned content and regularly maintained a website. If you are able to optimize your site in a manner that is favored by Google and easy for the users to browse, then retaining a higher rank wouldn't be a challenge for you. See online resource on how to get page 1 ranking using our online academy, which is *FREE for the users of this book.*

The only requirement you need to fulfill in this strategy is to remain consistent in your efforts to improve your ranking.

Tracking and maintaining your business listings on the Google My Business page can guarantee you high online position.

The content you post on your website should relate to your target audience. It should provide users the answers they are looking for. If you are able to achieve this, you'd be ultimately able to dominate the Google Maps Ranking easily.

Google Keyword Planner Tool

https://ads.google.com/home/tools/keyword-planner/

How to Be Higher on Google Search Results &

Outrank Your Local Competitors

Most wise business owners are always studying what their best competitor is doing when it comes to the Google search. However, most un-ethical SEO's are always finding ways to do SEO that works sometimes but it will end up risking the website.

I have had an experience helping clients who came to me when their websites were either de-indexed by Google or lost page 1 rankings and slipped to page 3 and onwards.

Since, I have been doing SEO for over 20 years working with the top SEO experts like Eric Ward, Bruce Clay, I always take a KISS approach. Keep super simple for search.

Don't try to be smarter than "Google."

Based on my own experience working with over 1000+ VIP brands, law firms, small business owners all over the world, I recommend that if you follow these methods, you will always be safe and trusted by big "G".

Accelerate Mobile Traffic with Accelerated Mobile Pages

Do you know the fact that with a speed loading website you can attract the users and increase their usability on your web pages and enormously improve customer conversions?

Huge Increase in Usage of Mobile Devices

It's a very well-known fact that Mobile Internet users are enormously increasing all over the nation and around the world. Having faster loading mobile web pages not only reduces the website loading time but also boosts Search engine rankings and increases the customer conversions. Is your website loading faster on the Mobile Devices?

Don't Lose a Visitor

A slow loading website discourages its users from browsing its content; leading to decrease the usability of the website, increasing the user bounce rates and abandonment. This results in a fall of conversion rate. Don't let the slow web pages kill your conversion rate.

Accelerated Mobile Pages can help!

It's quite important for your web pages to load faster to provide the best user experience, increase conversion rate and rank well on Google for mobile search. Accelerated Mobile Pages (also known as AMP) helps your web pages to load quickly for mobile users and gives a faster mobile browsing experience to your users. AMP or Accelerated Mobile Pages is an open source HTML proposal by Google.

"As per Google Support: Accelerated Mobile Pages (AMP) is an open source initiative that allows you to create web pages that load quickly on mobile browsers. To help provide a better mobile user experience, you can create AMP versions of your landing pages.

As per Google Support: Your landing page speed can make the difference between converting or losing a customer. Most mobile site visitors leave a page that takes more than 3 seconds to load. Yet most mobile sites miss that mark by an average of 19 seconds (Source). To set yourself apart from the competition, optimize your landing page experience with AMP.

Faster landing pages typically lead to more conversions, and AMP allows you to create pages that load quickly without compromising creativity and brand expression. Combining speed and smoother loading, AMP landing pages often give people much better landing page experiences. AMP loads quickly because it's designed for speed."

Light Weighted Web Pages Loads Faster!

The lightweight web pages load faster on mobile devices with smooth scrolling, speed loading content, faster transitions and animations, quickly loaded info-graphics and videos, all other content loading quickly! Accelerated Mobile WebPages are light weighted web pages and are greatly set for speed, smooth functioning, and make it much easier to be loaded on mobile devices.

Google Map Citations

A Google Map citation is actually just a mention of your business name, address, and phone number on another website. For instance, an example of a citation could be a business directory such as Yelp, Foursquare, or Yahoo Local, where your company is mentioned by name.

Local citations don't need to include a link to your website. However, the greater the number of reputable citations you can acquire, the higher Google will rank your GMB listing and website. As part of a bonus, I have provided a list of web directories where you can secure citations from.

Data Accuracy

It's extremely important you post the same phone number, address and business name consistently in all business directories and citations (i.e. mentions of your name, address and phone number) as that helps your map listing rank higher in local map searches. Name, address, phone number (NAP) consistency is paramount. When the NAP is inconsistent, Google robot will crawl all consistent and wrong listings. Inconsistent listings will cause your MAP not to show.

Ranking Factors

Citations are used to help rank your Google+ Local map listing by supplying reputable sources of information about your business. Google validate these aspects:

Your business actually exists

It is a legitimate business

Your business description is accurate and corroborated by several sources

When Google sees information about your company on other websites and directories, this compels them to be more confident about the information you have provided in the description of your business. This ensures that Google is more likely to display your business listing when a person performs a search for the types of products or services you offer and promote.

However, in order for you to take full advantage of your local citations, it's imperative you set up a Google+ Local Business Page, claim your business. Then, optimize it by getting your business name and details added to directories and other web pages.

Citation Types

Here's a (non-exhaustive!) list of citation types.

Business directories (Yellow Pages, Yelp, Kudzu etc.)

Industry, niche or sector specific directories (Trip Advisor, Connecting Dance)

Local newspaper and press websites

Local themed blogs

Prominent local websites (particularly if they're related to your business niche)

Social Profiles (Twitter, FourSquare, Facebook, YouTube)

Beat Competitors with Citations

To beat your competition with citations you essentially need more high-quality citations than your competitor has. While total numbers are important, it's also crucial you keep in mind that the quality of the directory on which the citation is hosted, is high and the information you enter is accurate.

The more complete your general and niche citations are, the more value they will create towards ranking your Google+ Local listing and improving your visibility and presence within the Google maps products overall.

While business-listing citations are relatively easy to obtain, the more difficult ones come from local or niche websites and even local newspapers. You need to have something that is newsworthy for the media to talk about and get their attention.

Attract Attention with Local Citations

A great local citation needs to be seen as credible and trustworthy by people and Google. Brands like Yellow Pages (Yell) or Thompson Local are great places to start.

Make sure you fill out 3 pieces of crucial information. These must also be present on your website as selectable HTML text and not a graphic. Company name (*This should ideally be your branded trading name*)

A local telephone number with a local area code

The physical address of your business

If a local newspaper covers your business story, they are unlikely to display your company address or telephone number. In this case, having your company clearly referenced by name in order for your listing to receive full value is enough.

Google My Business Competitive Edge Features

Google My Business Questions (Q&A) and Answers - This allows your customers to ask you a question directly within your business listing. The questions can range from specific queries about what you have to offer to nonsensical one-word comments or obvious questions about your store hours.

These inquiries can be up voted, which will play into how high each one will rank within your Q&A section. As a business owner, you can log into your Google Maps mobile app to respond to these questions or flag non-legitimate comments or complaints.

Descriptions - Business owners can now include a 750-character description of your business. You don't have to include a description that is lengthy, as it will get shortened, but at least provide a unique paragraph that describes your brand and what you sell.

Book Appointments - You can now take users directly to a landing page or area to book an appointment with you. These appointment URLs can be used for any kind of local business, from senior care communities to law firms to restaurants. Don't pass on taking people right to your landing/squeeze page.

Local Visibility System, LLC

Website

4.9 ★ ★ ★ ★ ★ 50 Google reviews
Internet marketing service in North Attleborough, Massachusetts

Address: North Attleborough, MA
Hours: Open today · Open 24 hours ▼
Phone: (508) 308-4040
Appointments: localvisibilitysystem.com

Suggest an edit

Google Posts - On Google Post, you can share your latest product release, upcoming event, or announcement through this feature. This is an easy way to share eye-catching images with 100-300-words. Go to your Google My Business dashboard and click on "posts" to upload a new posting for your business.

Press Releases and Your SEO - Having information about your company or an event published on big news sites is not only beneficial for your brand, but also for your SEO. If news publishers start talking about you, not only can you get backlinks from the news sites themselves, which hold a very high amount of equity, but you can also score a high number of backlinks from other webmasters who will read the news.

Most of you are aware that building backlinks is one of the most difficult tasks for SEO. However, building high quality backlinks is even harder. Fortunately, press releases combine all the 3 above, which makes it probably the best link building method available.

It's worth noting that a well-timed press release can start a chain reaction not only with backlinks, but also with social media likes, shares, and comments. When you have news, press releases will be a useful and potentially effective method to boost your Google ranking, while attracting traffic to your GMB listing and website.

Make Effective Press Releases

Have an interesting piece of news

Create a killer headline

Write the Press Release short and to the point

Distribute only to relevant places

Wait and monitor results

Press Release Ideas.

Bonus: As a bonus for readers of this, we will give each users who contacts us and shares receipt of this book, we will give a press release for "FREE" that will reach AP News, Fox, NBC News Affiliates and Google News.

50 Reasons to Send a Press Release

The opening of your business. Local media is particularly interested in new businesses, especially when they offer a helpful product or service for the community. Write your press release showing the benefits to your community and target market. You can even include a special offer or gift to encourage people to visit your business.

The launch of your website. The launch of a helpful website is newsworthy, just like the launch of a business. Make sure your release includes the useful features of your website. Invite readers to visit your website for a gift. It could be a white paper, report, coupon, software, tool, etc.

Change in product offering. If you're launching a new product that will help or if you're lowering your prices, this might just be very newsworthy. Just keep in mind how your target market benefits and make that the focus of your release.

Offering a new service. Sometimes retailers get into the service industry, and that is a great reason to issue a press release.

Additionally, if you're a service provider and you're launching a new service or service bundle, then a press release is in order.

Launching a membership program. Are you starting a membership program? Share what membership offers and how your audience benefits from this new program.

Joint ventures. If you're combining forces with another company or individual and it benefits your target market, share that information in a press release.

Association membership. Join your local Chamber of Commerce or another business association. Include information on how you're contributing to the group. Don't know what association to join? Create your own.

A business move If you're moving to a new location that provides additional benefits to your customers, write a release. For example, while you're new location gives you more room for inventory, moving to a location with its own parking lot or curbside parking, will help your customers. In the release, focus on how a previous parking issue and how the move will be beneficial to customers.

Share your expertise. Celebrate your business anniversary by sharing your knowledge or skills with customers. Invite the public to join you as you give lessons, hold a Q & A session, or organize an exhibit that highlights your skills and knowledge. In the press release, highlight the skills and information you plan to share with customers and how you'll do it.

Make a prediction. Use local or national buzz to make a prediction that resonates with your niche audience. Include supporting evidence, facts, and statistics for credibility in your press release. Evidence could include customer responses about what they think, feel, and/or the actions they take or plan to take.

Solve a problem. Is your target audience up in arms about an issue or problem? Create a solution and present it to them or provide an outlet for them to be heard. For example, if there has been an increase in teen incidents or crimes, JV with other businesses to work with parents and teens and teach teens the skills of your trades.

"Celebrities" that use your product. If a respected individual in your community or niche uses your product, share that news –

with their permission, of course. Include quotes from the "celebrity" that share why they came to you and the results they've received.

Capitalize on current events. A popular news story is the perfect tie into your release. If you can relate the story to your business, it is quite likely the media will be interested. For example, if there is an increase in home break-ins in the area and you sell home security systems, you can write a release that includes tips for securing a home that refers to your products.

Capitalize on pop culture. Popular TV shows, movies, and music are great beginning point for a press release. For example, if you teach music lessons a tie-in to the popular TV show, Glee might be an interesting angle.

Share your awards and accomplishments. If you've won an award or received some other type of recognition, this is perfect press release fodder. Show how this accomplishment serves your community/ target market.

Give awards. Not only can you share information about awards you receive, you can give out meaningful awards to your community as well.

Fundraiser donation. Spread awareness for your cause and your business, by holding a fundraiser. For more newsworthy exposure, make it a competition between your business and a friend's business.

Fundraiser follow-up. Be sure to follow-up the announcement of your upcoming fundraiser with a summary of the results you each achieved.

Be a sponsor. Sponsor a local team or organization and write a press release about it. It shows you contribute and support the community.

Have a contest. Whether you host a sweepstakes, essay, or video contest, it's fun and interesting to your audience. Make sure to send a follow-up when the winners are announced.

Host a special event. Put together an open house or customer appreciation day. Offer refreshments, helpful information, etc. to attendees. Let the media know about the event with a press release.

Host a virtual event. Organize a teleseminar or webinar that provides valuable information to your target customer and announce this free event through your press release.

Create a useful publication. Are you putting together a helpful newsletter, white paper, or report? Share an announcement about it in a press release. Be sure to explain why it is newsworthy for the public.

Create an internship or work experience program. If you're going to hire some students for the summer, share the news. Follow up with stories on the success of the program with some of your star participants.

Release a research report or study. As a company, if you gather information from your audience or industry, publish that information in a report and share it in a press release to announce your findings.

Announce your exhibit at a trade show or convention. Will you attend a conference or trade show? Issue a release before the event to share what is unique about your attendance at the event and what it means for the public and your customers.

Teach a class. Share the information that will be taught and the details of the class. Is it free? Who can take the class? Why is it being offered?

Announce an upcoming speaking engagement. Share what you'll be talking about, why you're speaking, and mention others, who will be speaking or attending. Include a little about why you'd like to "invite" the community or public to attend.

Pricing or policy changes. If you make any notable changes to your pricing, policies, or changes that benefit consumers, a press release explaining the details can help to build your brand, as well as increase traffic and sales.

Patents and trademarks. Did you recently trademark or patent something? That's big news. Share it in a press release.

Win a court case. Going to court isn't fun and usually it's not something to write about. However, if you win a notable court case, a press release can announce the information and you can deal with the situation head on.

Discover an innovative use for your products. Whether you've found an innovative use for your products or a customer shares it with you, this is something to share and a press release can help get the word out.

Announce new and notable clients you've obtained. Did you just sign a deal with a major company? Did Oprah just buy your product? Share the news in a press release.

Share first person stories about people using your product or services. The media loves to hear personal interest stories and it's a great way to help people connect with your brand.

Financial projections and announcements. If you're a publicly held company, you might issue a release when you have financial projections and forecasts to share.

Announce the retirement of well-known and respected employees. Share the love and issue a press release recognizing their accomplishments.

Recognize employees that give back to the community. Issue a press release celebrating a valued employee.

Highlight charitable donations by your company. If your company feels strongly about a charitable organization, partner with them to raise money, or make a donation. A press release is a terrific way to get attention for the organization, and to strengthen your brand.

Make a public statement on future business trends or conditions. Many industries do this on a regular basis. When an annual or quarterly report comes out, the company issues a release that highlights their position or how they're going to move forward given the new industry trends.

Recognize a leadership position. Announcing that an individual in your business has been named to serve in a leadership position in a professional or charitable organization.

Announce the launch of a social media initiative. Did you create a unique Facebook group or LinkedIn group that offers a benefit to members?

Announce that you've reached a major milestone. Has your company been in business for 25 years? Have you reached one million in sales? If you've reached a milestone, a press release can help you share the information and build your brand.

Discuss an expansion or renovation. If you're expanding or renovating your business, a press release can share the benefit of that expansion with your audience and the media.

Establish a unique agreement. Sometimes it's newsworthy to discuss any innovative agreements you make with customers or vendors. Highlight the benefit to your audience in the release. That's what people care about.

Share a story of perseverance. If your company has met a challenge or risen above adversity, it may resonate with the media as a personal interest story. Tell about the experience to inspire others.

Restructure. Restructuring your business or business model is newsworthy if you focus on the benefit for the consumer. For example, if you're changing from retailer to a subscription-based model the benefit for consumers may be that their product stays supported and up to date.

Announce a new certification. Some industries have certifications. Coaching is one example. Engineering and manufacturing are other examples. If you've received a new certification, issue a press release to announce it.

Announce a big sale. This type of press release is difficult to write because it must be newsworthy. Think about why you're having the sale (or create an interesting reason.) Maybe you're making room for new products, adding a new product line inspired by a customer, or maybe you're taking the business in a different direction.

Publish a book. If you've published a book or have a contract with a publisher to write a book, issue a press release and share the news.

Earned media coverage. This can be a delicate tightrope to walk. However, you can issue a press release, if you've earned media coverage from another publication. For example, if Consumer Reports rates your products as the best in your niche, you could issue a press release announcing that recognition.

25 Citation Sites

Acxiom - https://mybusinesslistingmanager.myacxiom.com/

Angie's List - http://www.angieslistbusinesscenter.com/

Apple Maps - https://mapsconnect.apple.com/

B2B Yellow Pages - http://www.b2byellowpages.com/

Bing Places - https://www.bingplaces.com/

City Search - http://www.citysearch.com/

Dun & Bradstreet - https://www.dnb.com/

eLocal - http://www.elocal.com/

Express Update - http://www.expressupdate.com/search

Facebook - https://www.facebook.com/bookmarks/pages

Factual - https://www.factual.com/data/t/places

Foursquare - https://foursquare.com/

Google My Business - https://www.google.com/business

Local - https://advertise.local.com/?CID=710

Make It Local - https://www.makeitlocal.com/

Manta - https://www.manta.com/

MapQuest - https://www.mapquest.com/

Merchant Circle - http://www.merchantcircle.com/

Neustar - https://www.neustarlocaleze.biz/directory/Search

Super Pages - http://www.superpages.com/

Yahoo! Local - https://search.yahoo.com/?fr=local_lyc_syc_rd

Yellow Book - http://www.yellowbook.com/

Yellow Pages - https://www.yellowpages.com/

Yelp - https://biz.yelp.com/

Zip Local - https://ziplocalonline.com/manage-listings

Online Reputation Defense Checklist

When it comes to battling negativity online and maintaining the integrity of your reputation, strategic defense and a good offense is the best policy. Use this checklist as a tool to assess what people are saying about you, create content to counteract any damage, maintain control of your online presence, and respond to negativity appropriately.

	Find Out What People are Saying About You Online
	Perform a Google search of your name
	Set up alerts to tell you when your name is mentioned
	Create a record of everything you find, and where it is
	Categorize items into positive and negative comments
	Identify repeated mentions of your natural strengths
	Identify which efforts you've been making that have paid off

	Identify any misunderstanding in the negative content you find
	Identify any truths in the negative content
	Decide whether each negative should be responded to or removed
	Make notes on what you can learn from each piece of negative content

	Create Positive Content to Counteract Negativity
	Identify which pieces of content you've produced previously were well received
	Identify the best places to reach your target market
	Identify the best types of content to reach your target market
	Include your branding on all pieces of content you create
	Create a schedule to plan release of content

	Interact with your audience when they make comments on your content
	Look for opportunities to provide your audience with more information or help
	Encourage reviews and testimonials and use them as positive content
	Create positive content associated with negative keywords as a proactive SEO campaign

AMP – A Great Framework

Google started AMP framework project, other major social media sites (such as Twitter and Pinterest) also incorporated AMP on their platforms. The websites integrated with AMP framework load faster on mobile devices. Without of all the overstuffed code, and needless things and with super fast loading, AMP web pages provide greater mobile browsing experience to its users and get the outstanding results by increasing the users usability.

Even though they are mainly designed for mobile devices (as the name suggests they are accelerated mobile pages), the web pages can also be made to be responsive, and work on desktops as well, and based on that they have completely exceptional presentation results.

Create your AMP HTML page

"As per pbakaus & amp.dev [3] Create your AMP HTML page:

The following markup is a decent starting point or boilerplate. Copy this and save it to a file with a .html extension.

```
<!doctype html>
<html amp lang="en">
 <head>
 <meta charset="utf-8">
 <script async
src="https://cdn.ampproject.org/v0.js"></script>
 <title>Hello, AMPs</title>
```

```
<link rel="canonical"
href="https://amp.dev/documentation/guides-and-
tutorials/start/create/basic_markup/">
    <meta name="viewport" content="width=device-
width,minimum-scale=1,initial-scale=1">
    <script type="application/ld+json">
{"@context": "http://schema.org", "@type": "NewsArticle",
"headline": "Open-source framework for publishing content",
"datePublished": "2015-10-07T12:02:41Z", "image": [
"logo.jpg" ] }
    </script>
<style amp-boilerplate>body{-webkit-animation:-amp-start 8s
steps(1,end) 0s 1 normal both;-moz-animation:-amp-start 8s
steps(1,end) 0s 1 normal both;-ms-animation:-amp-start 8s
steps(1,end) 0s 1 normal both;animation:-amp-start 8s
steps(1,end) 0s 1 normal both}@-webkit-keyframes -amp-
start{from{visibility:hidden}to{visibility:visible}}
@-moz-keyframes -amp
start{from{visibility:hidden}to{visibility:visible}}
```

```
@-ms-keyframes -amp-
start{from{visibility:hidden}to{visibility:visible}}@-o-
keyframes -amp-
start{from{visibility:hidden}to{visibility:visible}}@keyframes -
ampstart{from{visibility:hidden}to{visibility:visible}}</style><
noscript><style amp-boilerplate>body{-webkit-
animation:none;-moz-animation:none;-ms-
animation:none;animation:none}</style></noscript>
</head>
 <body>
<h1>Welcome to the mobile web</h1>
</body>
</html>
```

The content in the body, so far, is pretty straightforward. But there's a lot of additional code in the head of the page that might not be immediately obvious. Let's deconstruct the required mark-up.

Use HTTPS: When creating AMP pages and content, you should strongly consider using the HTTPS protocol (vs. HTTP). Although, HTTPS is not required for the AMP document itself or for images and fonts, there are many AMP features that require HTTPS (e.g., video, iframes, and more). To ensure your AMP pages take full advantage of all AMP features, use the HTTPS protocol."

It makes Difference

The website loading speed can make all the difference between losing and converting the users of your web pages. The majority of mobile users visiting websites on their devices will leave a web page that takes longer than three seconds to load. Optimizing your website with Accelerated Mobile Pages reduces these bounce rates.

Accelerated Mobile Pages VS Responsive Web Design

Most website owners are confused with Responsive Web Design and Accelerated Mobile Pages. They aren't the same; Accelerated Mobile Pages are different from the responsive web design on its benefits on faster mobile browsing. The impact of bounce rate on search engine rankings is somewhat high.

AMP reduces these bounce rates enormously.

- Even though Accelerated Mobile Pages and Responsive websites both work on mobile devices, they vary in terms of some functioning, benefits and their goals.

- Accelerated Mobile Pages are focused on fast loading and it is set up for delivering web page content quickly/ instantly to the mobile users; Whereas responsive websites are focused on flexibility.

- Accelerated Mobile Pages framework can be integrated easily on the existing/normal website without re-designing the existing website; but a normal website has to be re-designed to make it Responsive Website.

- Compared to Responsive websites the Accelerated Mobile Pages load twice faster!

Benefits of Accelerated Mobile Pages

- Easy to incorporate without re-design

- Speed Loading

- User attractive

- Accessible on both Mobile devices and desktops

- Reduced Bounce rate

- Best Mobile Browsing Experience
- Increased User Usability and Engagement
- More Conversions
- Highly supports Google Ads
- Improves keyword rankings on mobile search
- Utilization for High authority backlinks
- Useful, reliable and quality oriented

For faster loading web pages, better user experience on mobile devices and to increase mobile search engine ranking and high customer conversion rate, AMP framework is absolutely necessary for a website and there is no doubt about it.

You might want to consider help from experts to incorporate Accelerated Mobile Pages framework to your existing website and improve your Web pages users' usability on mobile devices. KISS PR expert team can help you right from scratch till delivering you desired results.

Source Links:

https://support.google.com/googleads/answer/7384020?hl=en

https://support.google.com/googleads/answer/7496737?hl=en

https://amp.dev/documentation/guides-and-tutorials/start/create/basic_markup/?format=websites

	Maintain Control
	Create a profile on every social media platform your market uses
	Plan to check in and interact at least once a day on each
	Be aware of privacy settings of each platform and keep an eye out for changes
	Post only relevant, appropriate content
	Monitor how each piece of content you post is received
	If you haven't already, register your business's domain name and your own
	Set up automatic renewal for when it expires
	Create a business email address

	Keep your personal and business email addresses separate
	Include a contact form on your website for people to contact you
	Check website content regularly to make sure it's up-to-date
	Make sure all of your content conforms to your brand message

	Deal with Negativity Accordingly
	Brainstorm scenarios where you might receive negative content
	Make a plan for dealing with each
	Ask your team members for input and look at comments you've received in the past
	Identify where negativity is coming from
	Identify if negativity is genuine or not

	If it's inappropriate or an obvious troll, delete it or ask the webmaster to remove it
	If you feel it's a genuine comment then respond
	Ask for more information
	Empathize
	Don't apologize until you understand the whole situation
	If it is your fault then apologize sincerely
	Offer a reasonable and realistic solution

Essential Tools for Managing Your Online Reputation

Google Alerts - A customized search that will notify you whenever new content is added that matches keywords that you've specified.

Hootsuite Insights – Analytics for understanding social media conversations regarding your brand.

If this Then That – Automate response tasks according to mentions of keywords assigned by you.

Mention – Monitor different areas online and response directly via the tools' interface.

TalkWalker Alerts – A widely used alternative to Google Alerts

KISSPR – A tool for monitoring and managing your listings on location and review sites

KISS PR Story – A press release company for improving your reputation.

Buzzsumo – A variety of different alert types, including the ability to email you whenever a link is added somewhere that points at your site

Moz Fresh Web Explorer – Great for metrics and will let you know immediately whenever anyone makes an unlinked mention of your business

Ahrefs – Another great tool for backlink notification, web mentions and keyword tracking

Complaint Search Box – Search all complaints websites at once for mentions of your business

Build a Google Knowledge Panel Using Press Release Distribution

If you want to know how to get your brand or business quickly noticed and indexed by the Google Knowledge Graph and improve your brand visibility, then you have arrived at the right destination.

Types of Google Results

Google displays different types of search results on page one depending on the search queries, such as organic search results, Google Maps 3 pack results, Google Business Listing, Google Knowledge Graph results, featured snippets (bullet list, number list, table list), Google Ads, Rich Answers, Google Answers boxes, videos and images results.

Google Info-box on Search Results

People love and expect to see quick, accurate and relevant results easily at a glance when they search for anything on search engines. Search engines collect relevant authority data from a variety of sources all over the internet and make more focused and accurate data available to its visitors on its search results. Google provides different types of info-boxes on its relevant search results in response to visitors' search queries; this helps the visitors to discover the corresponding information that goes along with a person's profile, organization, business products or services, brand, company profile, etc. For example, if you Google my name, you will see my knowledge panel.

Help Google to Send You More Qualified Traffic

Google has a great feature that allows you to explore more about you, your brand or anything that you like to explore or market on the internet. If you need more qualified traffic from Google, then it's time to help Google to build a knowledge database about YOU or your brand and your business products or services.

In order to help Google to help you find the right information about display your expertise, authority and trust (EAT), you have to feed the right kind of data that can be stored in the database, so Google neatly formats this data in the form of a knowledge info-box, thus providing this knowledge-based info-boxes on its relevant search results in response to visitors' search queries. As long as you do this consistently, Google keeps sending more traffic to you. I have outlined the steps to get you started. I do want to caution you that the knowledge panel is a single of "trust," and it is no so easy to adopt ethical search engine optimization.

For Google to generate a Knowledge Graph about your brand, first, you need to get your brand discovered and identified by Google. It gathers information from authoritative sources and consolidates this information in the form of info-boxes and displays on its search results.

How Do You Get a Google Knowledge Panel?

"As per Marieke van de Rakt. *What is a Knowledge Panel?* Google's Knowledge Panel is the block you'll find on the right side of your screen in the search results. Nowadays, you'll see it for a lot of queries. It presents the results of Google's Knowledge Graph, which can be seen as an engine connecting all kinds of data Google finds on the web. If you have a local, branded or personal panel, you might be able to influence what Google shows in the panel.

"Knowledge Panels are a type of rich results in Google's search results pages. They can show information about all kinds of things: businesses, people, animals, countries or plants, for instance. Such a panel appears on the right side of your screen in the desktop search results. It shows details on the particular entity you're searching for. What you see in this panel is powered by Google's Knowledge Graph."

What is Google Knowledge Graph?

Google search has a great feature that allows you to discover more than just what you are looking for; this mainly works when you are trying to find or research any information on famous brands or well-known people. For example, let's say you want to find information on Michael Phelps (the world's top swimmer); the Google-search results give you a snippet of text that describes him and some background information, and they also show other authority information about him and similar searches for people like Michael Phelps. So, the results also show different types of medals that he has won and similar swimmers or other famous swimmers that are very similar to Michael Phelps.

So, let's say you wanted to find a gold medal; you could click on it, and then, at the top (this is called a knowledge bar), it allows you to scroll and look at lots of different gold medals that Michael Phelps has won; this makes it really quick and easy for you to do more research on Michael Phelps.

Create a Google Knowledge Panel

Per Google Support

How to Get Verified on Google

Note: If you're verified as an authorized representative of your organization, you'll see a box at the top of the organization's knowledge panel. This box allows you to suggest edits to the knowledge panel. Verification also allows some to participate in Google Posts.

If you're a local business that serves customers at a particular location or within a designated service area, join Google My Business to manage your presence on Google search results and Google Maps.

How to Get Verified

To verify that you're an authorized representative for the entity, follow the steps below:

Ensure that you have a Google account. If you don't, then create a Google account.

Go to Google Search

Search for yourself or the entity you represent and find its knowledge panel. Scroll to the bottom and click "Claim this knowledge panel."

Review the displayed information about features granted after verification.

Sign in to one of the official sites or profiles listed to verify that you're an authorized representative of an entity on Google.

The list includes the following options:

• YouTube

• Search Console

• Twitter

• Facebook

After you sign in successfully, you can manage the entity on Google.

How to Get into the Knowledge Graph

Use Schema Markup to Tag Your Website Elements

With the implementation of schema markup on your website, you can make it a lot easier for Google to read the content/information on all of your web pages. This is a great advantage that improves your chances of getting into the Google Knowledge Graph and getting found on the rich snippets and info-boxes that are shown by Google in its search results. To build a website with the correct schema, talk to a KISS PR SEO Expert. (https://kisspr.com/seo)

Create Google My Business and Local Listings

A Google My Business (GMB) listing is one of the easiest and quickest ways to get straight into the Google Knowledge Graph. This Local Knowledge Graph result appears on the top-right side of Google's search results when searched with any business, organization, or brand name.

- Create a Google My Business profile (it's free!).

- Make sure your NAP (Name, address, and phone number) is consistent.

- Provide as much information as you can on your GMB profile.

- Enhance your social media accounts on GMB.

- Integrate your website blog on GMB.

- Provide accurate, relevant and current information of your business on GMB.

- Post appealing and engaging assets (content, HD photos, short videos).

- Get more reviews from customers.

- Respond to customer reviews and questions.

- Improve interactions with customers.

- Publish blog content to your GMB.

- Perform content-based local SEO.

Local Listings/Citations

Post your business listing (with the same NAP that you already have submitted to your Google My Business profile) to high authority local directories and other major search engines like Bing Places, Yahoo Local and Yelp. Make sure to maintain consistency with your NAP.

Reach with Press Releases

Authoritative press releases are considered official statements released to news sites and the media on behalf of any entity. The purpose of a press release is to represent the latest news about you or your brand through online media, officially to the general people, your target audience and existing customers. https://story.kisspr.com/

Representing your profile, brand, business or organization with an official press release not only builds trust of your brand but also attracts Google Knowledge Graph. Google pulls the required reliable and official news about any entity from famous news sites, high-authority journals and media sources. It is more likely that the news will appear in Google's News section or in the rich-text section.

Post Your Story on Wikipedia

As an authoritative and reliable content information resource on the internet, Wikipedia is the most trusted source by Google. With the help of Wikipedia, you can easily get your information straight into the Google Knowledge Graph. Create a page and post your story on Wikipedia as it helps your content become well-recognized and frequently pulled up by Google.

Do a little research before creating the content on Wikipedia; learn how the Wikipedia community works because information and tips help your content get approved sooner and ensures your page won't be removed or de-listed while under review by the Wikipedia team.

Create an Article Page on Wikidata

Wikidata is another highly trusted open-source on the internet that provides reliable content and authoritative information to its users. Improve your brand visibility and awareness with optimized Wikidata content. Create a Wikidata page and easily get your brand story into the Google Knowledge Graph through it.

Create and Enhance Social Media Accounts

Promote your brand, business or profile on Google Knowledge Graph with your official social media profiles. Social media icons like Facebook, Twitter, LinkedIn, Instagram, YouTube and Pinterest can appear on Google Knowledge Panel. These social media icons also appear on Google My Business listing as well. Knowledge Panel info-box for a brand, business, company or organization typically appears either on the top right-hand side or at the top of the Google Page 1 search results. Adding social media profiles to your Google Knowledge Graph can build your brand's trust, improve brand image and increase followers; linking these social media accounts to your website also improves your website's domain authority.

Since Google displays social profile links in their Knowledge Graph results, it is suggested to have at least four major social media accounts (Facebook, Twitter, LinkedIn, YouTube or Instagram) set-up for Google Knowledge Graph.

Approach Using Content Strategy

Providing reliable, informative, and useful content for your users is the key to attracting presentation by the Google Knowledge Graph. The content that you provide on your website should always be knowledge-based and user-engaging.

Integrate Keywords

Integrate target keywords in your page titles, meta descriptions, header titles, sub-headings, image tags, FAQs, introductions, and conclusions. Make sure, though, not to stuff these factors with keywords.

Provide a Questions-and-Answers Section

Create a questions-and-answers section on your website; make sure to provide answers for all questions your users are likely to ask. Avoid providing questions and answers that are overly long or overly short. Single-sentence questions and answers are advisable. This type of user-friendly content attracts Google, creating a high chance of selection for the Google Knowledge

Graph and placement on the first page of search results. Make sure to put target keywords in the questions and answers.

Set Up a YouTube Channel

Help Google gather your brand, business, or organization information through YouTube videos. Create a YouTube video channel with your promotional videos and embed these videos on your website and social media accounts as well. Depending on the search query, Google may show your video in the search results.

Post HD Infographics and Images

You have the opportunity to see your images and infographics placed on the Google Knowledge Card. Create an Info-graphic or Image representing your story and tag it with your target keyword. You can implant this infographic on your web pages, blog, content sources, social media accounts, and other high-authority sources.

Create More Social Media Profiles

There are many high-authority websites, directories and social media sites out there that allow you to create your profile on them. You can create your authoritative profiles on these sites.

This will help Google to gather more information about you or your brand from these sources and show them on its Knowledge Graph.

Make sure the information you submit or post on the internet is reliable, accurate and consistent. Inconsistent data will confuse Google, and it will challenge your efforts to get into the Google Knowledge Graph.

Get Your Brand Story Straight into the Google Knowledge Graph with the Help of the KISS PR expert team!

Getting your brand story into the Google Knowledge Graph isn't a simple task; it requires a lot of patience and expertise. Sometimes the whole process seems to be quite challenging. Let the team of Google Knowledge Graph experts from the KISS PR help you in this process right from scratch until you see the results!

Source Links:

https://yoast.com/all-about-googles-knowledge-panels/

https://support.google.com/knowledgepanel/answer/7534902?hl=en

About the Author

Qamar Zaman an American entrepreneur is a founder of KISS PR Story, a digital media, SEO, and press release company dedicated to the needs of business owners, entrepreneurs, and executives. Zaman has been featured in many top tier news publications an expert website growth expert. His advice has been featured in major publications such as Forbes, Chamber of Commerce, and the Caymanian Press.